Odyssey of a Soul in Bondage

*The story of one man's journey
out of the spiritual prison of psychological
and emotional bondage.*

Jon E. Quick

Research and Information Services
Bend, Oregon

Published in the United States of America by
Research and Information Services, Inc.

http://www.workersect.org/

Library of Congress Control Number: 2007942144
ISBN: 978-0-9639419-5-4

For the three most precious people in my life:
Trisha, Jenna, & Marissa

You deserve so much more, but perhaps this
book will bring you understanding and
answers. Understanding and answers, of
which I was totally lacking, in the time I was
blessed to be a part of your lives.

Love always, Dad

Dedication

Dedicated to Mr. Bob Daniel, who left this world in April 2004.

Bob, you were the first of "them" to write to me, and subsequently the first to encourage me to use my circumstances to reach out to others. For this reason, I have written, and now dedicate, this book to your memory.

Thank you, Bob. You will always be remembered.

Table of Contents

Odyssey of a Soul in Bondage

Foreword

Our actions are influenced by our environments, our upbringings, the friends and associates we choose, and our families. Yet, our actions also are a profound statement of the persons we have decided to become. How we react is predicated on our choices — whether with honesty or with deception, with reason or with violent passion, with open-mindedness or with prejudice, with love which focuses outward, or with hatred which makes an idol of self.

Even the influences on our lives are a series of choices, some accepted with difficulty, some assimilated so easily as to go unnoticed, some unquestioningly received — being built upon a foundation of previous choices and influences, good or bad.

But, for the most part, we do not examine the impact of the steps we take towards creating the person we are. One can live one's life in a cocoon of sorts — surrounded by the unquestioned, self-centered "rightness" of the preconceptions and prejudices that we have acquired, or even fostered — unless, and until, forced to take a serious look at the person one has built, choice upon choice.

What we decide to do on those occasions where we are forced to account for our choices, is yet another decision. We can take the opportunity to examine how we arrived at this point, and make course corrections. Or we can fall into blaming others for our decisions, blaming circumstances, blaming God, bemoaning fate, blaming anything and everything in order to avoid facing and addressing the actual problems buried within ourselves — things we've chosen, or allowed, to become a part of our character.

It is a tendency within all of us to assume that we aren't selfish (or at least trying not to be), that the factors which we use in our judgments are sound in essence, that our decisions are basically altruistic and for (or toward) the good, that the information we have accepted as truths are accurate, that we are striving for the best. And these assumptions are seldom examined or challenged.

It is only when God holds up a mirror to ourselves that we tend to take time to even notice who we have become. For some of us, it might be when caught cheating or in a lie. For others it might occur when one of our assumptions crumbles before the facts. For another it might be consciousness of hurt caused to another. And for yet someone else, it might be a financial or personal crisis. Mr. Quick has been forced into that self-examination in a most extreme way. What follows is not an excuse for what he allowed himself to become; it is an examination of the influences, choices and steps that have marked his path.

And while it may be that most readers will find it difficult to identify with Mr. Quick's experiences, we each have our own peculiar trail of preconceptions, pressures, motivations and influences which bear examining, and watchful accounting in our decisions, actions and judgments.

Each of us, in one manner or another, must eventually confront the person we have chosen to become.

— Kevin N. Daniel

"As it is written, There is none righteous, no, not one: There is none that understandeth, there is none that seeketh after God. They are all gone out of the way, they are together become unprofitable; there is none that doeth good, no, not one."
— Romans 3: 10-12.

"But we are all as an unclean [thing], and all our righteousnesses [are] as filthy rags; and we all do fade as a leaf; and our iniquities, like the wind, have taken us away." — Isaiah 64:6.

Odyssey of a Soul in Bondage

Acknowledgments

This book would not have been possible, without the tremendous positive influence I've received from a number of different people. Christine, when many others who once called themselves my friend showed their true colors by turning tail, you showed the colors of true friendship, and still remain, the truest friend I've ever known on this earth. Jim, Winston, and Pastor Milo, your unselfish dedication to the plight of those in undesirable circumstances planted a seed in my heart. Tom O., you encouraged me to study His Word like never before. Leonard R., though you don't share my faith in the Grace of God, you put the most important article of my life into my hands. William BeVier and the rest at RAS, you provided a major link and catalyst in opening the most important doors in my life.

Bob and Joan Daniel, Lori MacGregor, Rita McCormick, Rev. Jackson Buick, Don & Kathy Lewis, Dr. Ronald Enroth, Mary Ann Schoeff, and Lynn Cooper & Don Smith: you provided me with words and letters of encouragement, and tremendously helpful and insightful publications, which truly aided in the opening of the eyes of my heart and soul. Wes N. and Terry J., you both provided me with vital counseling; and while the counseling from each has been of a different nature, it's been spiritually and emotionally therapeutic.

Dr. Gene DeVoll and Doug Draper, you shared your similar experiences with me — experiences in life and in faith — and you began to encourage me to write. See what you started? Charlie and Ardis, you put up with many of my bizarre requests without complaint, and also gave me a listening ear on many occasions.

Last, but not least, Mary Jo. You entered my life at a very troubled time for myself, only to see me virtually vanish from yours without warning. In spite of this, unbeknownst to you, you provided me with the last little bit of inspiration and bravery I needed to take this leap of faith and write my story.

To all of you, thank you from the bottom of my heart, and may the blessing of the LORD be upon you, and upon any others which I may have inadvertently forgotten to mention.

Introduction

Now being in the 36th year and 11th month of my life, I feel the compelling need to attempt to explain what brought me to where I am today. In this writing, I would also like to enlighten many of my family and acquaintances to those things of which I have now become aware. I was convicted of first degree pre-meditated murder thirty-four years, one month, and eighteen days after I was born. As our modern system of justice often prematurely assumes, a straight and simple path leads from birth to crime, to punishment, as some people are just "bad."

This is a condensed, autobiographical account of my life history. Of many things contained herein, I have only rarely, if ever, spoken. Some of these memories I had not recalled until very recently. In attempting to keep this account condensed, I only mention those incidents which I feel to be particularly significant in bringing me to where I am today.

If, perchance, I have offended anyone by anything I have written herein, I apologize. For no offense has been intended. I must, however, defend the narrative which I have committed to these pages by stating the following: To keep the unadulterated truth cloaked in fog, due to any fear of offending someone, is to deprive communication of any real and living substance.

My friend, very few things in life are simple. And, in my own case, the route from birth to the present has led me through some very treacherous paths and experiences. But let me start at the beginning, for, after all, is that not where everything once started?

Odyssey of a Soul in Bondage

Part 1

The Beginning

"In the beginning God created the heavens and the earth. The earth was without form, and void, and darkness was on the face of the deep. And the spirit of God was hovering over the face of the waters."
— Genesis 1:1-2.

"In the beginning was the word, and the word was with God, and the word was God. He was in the beginning with God. All things were made through Him, and without Him nothing was made that was made." — John 1:1-3.

I was born on the 28ᵗʰ of August 1967, at 7:29 p.m.,[1] the youngest of eight, with five older sisters and two older brothers. My early recollections of childhood are quite spotty, the earliest events I can remember being that of waking up in the early evening, to a house that seemed to be empty. This, of course, being the old house located near the end of the black-top, five miles north of Audubon — or,

---

1 *I mention the time with a sense of accomplishment and pride, as until I began writing this autobiography, I had been unable to find out the time of day I was born. When asked on numerous occasions, my parents were never able to recall the time of my birth, and never deemed it*

in other words, just a mile or two past the middle of nowhere. I can still remember the wind whipping through the trees outside the living room window, and the ominous greenish tinge to the sky that usually indicated the approach of threatening weather. As a child of only three or four years of age, waking up alone in such a house was a truly terrifying experience, to say the least. I cannot recall to this day whether someone came in response to my wailing cries, or if I just cried myself back to sleep.

Terrifying as this was, those times I did not wake up to an empty and quiet house were, in many ways, even more terrifying. Here, I am using recollections mainly from the ages of four until around seven or eight.

I would wake up to hear my dad hollering at one of my sisters or my brother. He was usually angry because he thought they slept too late. This hollering was usually followed by smacks or screams, or a variety of other sounds which were especially unpleasant to the ears of a small child. On one occasion, I got up from the bed in bewilderment to ask what was going on, only to have my dad respond by marching over to me, slapping me viciously

---

worthwhile to take the trouble of providing an answer for me.

across the face with a wet washcloth, and telling me to quit "sassing."[2]

It was about this time we learned in school that "dad" meant the same as "father." This caused me some bewilderment, as every Sunday morning, Wednesday night, and other times of the week at *Gospel Meetings*, I would hear *friends* and *workers* begin their prayers with "Our father." It was hard to imagine **loving** this person they called "father," but it was not at all difficult to imagine *fearing* such a person. Needless to say, as I grew up, my fear of God was much stronger than my love for God.

There is one incident I recall from about the age of six. Two older sisters and an older brother were still in school, so they had not moved away from home yet. I was headed out to catch the bus in the morning. I recall only one sister was riding the bus from our family, as the other two were riding in my brother's car. And, as best I can recollect, I was part way out through the front yard, and for some reason, I needed to go back to the house. I forget the exact cause — whether there was a dead animal lying near the end of the driveway (I was deathly

---

2 *It was many years later that I realized how hard of hearing my father was. This hearing impairment led to us often being accused of saying things we did not say.*

scared of dead animals when I was little), or whether I had messed my pants somehow. But when I turned back toward the house, my dad started hollering at me. In my memory, I recall him picking up a chunk of firewood and threatening to beat me with it (or probably, more specifically, to pull my pants down and spank me with it — a very frequent threat of his) if I did not get going and catch the bus. Everything else regarding this incident is a big blank. I never even had any recollection of this occurrence until January of 2004, although I may have retained some memory of the event for a short while afterwards.

In April, 1976, at the age of eight, my mom and dad and two older sisters moved from that place two miles past the middle of nowhere, to a smaller place three miles east of Audubon. I always remember one thing that bothered me was how on Sunday mornings my father seemed to be such a Godly man (at least once we got to *meeting*), but that the rest of the week it seemed like he was a living demon. Or, I wondered, might it be that I am such a bad kid, that I provoke such anger and wrath from such a Godly man? He would often quote the scripture passage, *"Children obey your parents,"* and I often wanted to ask him about the part just after that, which says, *"Fathers, provoke not your children to wrath."* But having been instructed from a very early age to never question my elders, I never did.

Another reason I usually withheld saying anything to my dad was that, during the summer of 1976 or 1977, I did voice my displeasure about the way he was treating (abusing) one or two of my sisters. My disapproval was not expressed using the greatest of tact, though the result would have likely been quite similar, regardless. My dad promptly took me to the back portion of the front yard and proceeded to whip me across the bare butt with a large chunk of firewood. During this beating, my dad went on to yell at me that one of the *workers* thought I was an awful boy. This statement fed the notion that perhaps I was just a rotten kid. But, quite apart from the issue of whether I was good or bad, a feeling deep within me of pure hatred toward my father began to fester.

The notion that I just might actually be a bad kid may have made such negative feelings more acceptable in my own young and impressionable mind. However, this also added to the degradation of my self-esteem, as every time I would start feeling hateful toward my father, I would rationalize in my mind that it was acceptable for a "bad kid" to hate his father. After all, how could someone who seemed to have the *workers'* approval be a bad person? It *had* to be me, especially if *workers* thought I was an awful boy as well.

This new habit of maintaining silence was well assimilated by the time I witnessed another horrific event during the next year. My mom and dad were outside arguing in front of the shed, while my older sister Arlis and I watched from just inside the screen door. We didn't say a word to each other, but sensed the disposition of my dad growing more heated with the passage of each eternal moment. Suddenly without warning, my dad grabbed an axe, and while taking off after my mom with axe raised, spoke these words to my mom as though they came from the depths of Hell and Satan himself: *"Get out of here before I chop your bully head off!"*

Arlis gasped in surprise. I, in my recollection, remained much like "the night before Christmas, all through the house" — I didn't make a sound that I can remember, or perhaps it so short-circuited my mind that I became semi-unconscious (although I distinctly remember hearing Arlis let out that gasp). Next, I remember my mom running into the house, locking the front door, going around and trying to lock the back door, (the back door was very difficult to lock), and then proceeding to the phone. She called the sheriff's department.

I don't recall if I was still there when my dad came in the house. I have a vague recollection of him threatening to cut the phone cord, but I'm unsure whether that was on this occasion, or on one of many others. Anyway, I went down in the basement to my bedroom and laid down and went to sleep, as I felt there was nothing else I could do. I do remember, several hours later, overhearing Arlis tell our older sister Mary about the incident, as Mary had been at work and did not return home until later.

On my part, I never spoke one word of this incident until July of 2000, when I was going to marriage counseling. This, however, does not mean it was never thought of. It was a wound festering in the deepest recesses of my tormented soul. I no longer felt free to turn anything outward, so I only allowed my emotions to turn inward, to bear the damage where no one could see.

Through the late 1970's, I also endured some torment in school at Christmas time. Participation in Christmas programs was one thing my mom was totally against, as according to the *workers*, we did not need to be part of any *worldly* Christmas celebrations. With dread I would approach the teacher about the time of year we started practicing, to explain that I was not allowed to join in the Christmas program.

One year, in the third grade, I had an overly sympathetic teacher who, to my horror, insisted that I make absolutely certain that my mom would not permit me to do such a thing. Oh no! As if it wasn't bad enough having to tell my teachers, now I had to ask my mom. I would have gladly lied and told the teacher that I had asked her, but I was afraid that, in her misguided good intentions, she might call my mom and ask her herself.

From the moment I got home from school that day at 3:30, I set out to ask my mom the big question. Not "big" due to the uncertainty of her answer; big because I feared a severe lecture for not knowing the answer good and well without having to bother her with unnecessary questions. By the time I had worked up the nerve to ask her the question, it was about five hours later. I did it when we were busy carrying in groceries, as I knew in this way her mind would be preoccupied with something else, and I would hopefully be spared the "you should know better" lecture.

Well, I lucked out. She was busy enough that her response consisted only of a curt, "No, of course not." If I had really had my hopes up, I would have been devastated. But, instead, I was purely relieved to have this question put into the past. I guess you could say at this point, I knew better than to even *want* to be in the Christmas program.

This was just another element of *suffering for The Truth*.

During Christmas vacation of 1978, when I was eleven years of age, my father took me on a bus trip out west. I cannot say that I was forced into this. But Arlis and my mom both had jobs, and I felt pressured, almost as if I would be emulating the prodigal son if I didn't go. Once we were on the trip, I realized that my role was to be the one responsible to see that we didn't miss our bus at the larger bus terminals, as my dad was hearing impaired.

I also didn't find out until we were on the trip that many of the *friends* we stopped to see were not aware that we were coming. At the time this seemed a little odd, but I didn't figure out until years later that the reason for this was the bitter feud my father had gotten into earlier that year with the *elder* where we went to *meeting,* and subsequently, with some of the *workers*. He wanted a chance to catch everyone by surprise, so he could make his case without the *workers* getting the chance to excommunicate him before he could tell his side.

In looking back, I now realize that my dad was under an extreme amount of stress during these times. What made matters worse, was my mom's refusal to support him. As far as her considering a divorce, it would have been easier for her to allow my father to take her life, than for her to even think of such a thing. Yes, my mother would not leave my father for being dangerously abusive, yet she would not support him in his dispute with the *elder* where we went to *meeting*. The same reason was behind both of these factors. For her to lose favor with the *workers* would be unthinkable! Thus, she could not leave him, and she could not support him in his dispute with the *elder*. The latter, not because of what she believed was right or wrong, but simply because the *workers*, for the most part, chose to support the *elder*.

I had not realized until much later, but this flies right in the face of anything the Bible says about such things. She refused to protect her children, or herself, from a clearly abusive husband. Yet she also refused to support her husband in a dispute with someone outside the family, and allowed the words of men to dictate her loyalty to her husband.

This dispute also increased my dad's obsession[3] with making certain that my sisters and myself behaved at all times, as his approval by the *workers*

---

3 *Several years later, in 1988 or 1989, my father was diagnosed with an obsessive compulsive disorder.*

rested on very treacherous ground. This dispute, I believe, is also what started the argument leading up to the axe incident that I have already described.

Getting back to the trip out west, one particular couple of the *friends* that my dad visited in Los Angeles, had three of their grandchildren there. This was a delight for me, because very few of the *friends* my father stopped to see had kids anywhere near my age. One evening, while my dad and the man of the house were visiting, my dad's desperation for approval surfaced very sharply. The man of the house yelled out for his grandchildren to be quiet. My dad immediately commanded me to come over and sit at the table, not because I had done something wrong, but rather out of a fear that his own reputation might become tainted by any possible disapproval of my behavior.

The summer of 1979, or thereabouts, most of our family went up to Emo, Ontario for *convention*. I say most of our family, as my father, perhaps for reasons pertaining to his dispute with the *elder*, did not go. This, I in fact, looked forward to, as I did not find it enjoyable to be at *convention* with my father. For many years, he seemed to be obsessed that I would be the best behaved child at *convention*. This also included making certain I was the *first* child to go to bed each evening, sometimes as early as nine p.m. or ten minutes after, though we were "allowed" to be out until 10 p.m. This was in an environment where the parents of other children generally allowed them to stay out until about ten minutes to, or a quarter to ten.

As a result of his many restrictions, I was thrilled to be going to a *convention* without him. I believe it was the first night at Emo *Convention*, which would have been a Wednesday night, I went to bed on time, and then visited for awhile with two or three of my newfound friends in the dorm after the lights went out, as young boys will generally do. Sometime the following morning or afternoon, an older man came into the dorm and began visiting with several of us young boys. This man acted very friendly as we conversed, so when he finally asked us our names, we willingly told him.

My mother gave me the third degree later that day, as word had gotten back to her that there were some noisy young boys in the men's dorms the night before, and "Jon Quick" was the noisiest one. I was quite devastated by this, as I was truly attempting to be on my best behavior. But, as was generally the case, behavior of an eleven year old child was not acceptable from an eleven year old child. As I recall, my mother also made some mention that my dad would be very disappointed. I was also quite hurt that someone who acted so nice, such as this older man, would betray me. I made myself a promise that I would do my best to stay away from Emo *Convention,* as it was not our *home convention.* As it turned out, we moved to Idaho a couple of years later, and I never did go back to Emo *Convention.*

I didn't realize, until years later, that the only real purpose I ever served in my father's life was to act as a pawn in his quest for approval by the *workers and friends.* Even after my arrest in September of 2000, his primary reason for wanting to bail me out of jail was to bring me to *convention* so, as he hoped, I could *re-profess,* thus making my dad to appear as the most noble among the *saints* in the eyes of the *workers and friends.* This, my dear readers, is the epitome of "conditional love."

Arlis, my next older sister, graduated and left home in May of 1980. This left me to play the pawn game all by myself for the next six years. My father, and my mother to some extent, would focus their attention on molding each of their children into what they felt would bring them the greatest approval in the eyes of the *workers and friends.* This would begin once the child reached a certain age. But once the next child reached that certain age, they would then divert much of their molding to the younger child. As a result, each child seemed to reach a point where the burden of this molding process was relieved from their shoulders, and the object of these attentions were transferred to the next younger sibling, all the way down the line. However, what happens once there are no more younger siblings? You guessed it: not until after my horrific crime in September of 2000, and my subsequent refusal to accept any visits from my parents and some of my siblings, did I feel able to escape some of the never-ending intrusions into my private life by my father.

Yes, my last six years at home grew increasingly difficult. I suffered almost daily from migraine headaches. I grew increasingly moody and untalkative. I hardly ever spent time at home, and when one of my sisters came home for my high school graduation, I would hardly speak to her at any length. Yes, I was bitter toward my siblings, for I felt abandoned by them to the controlling clutches of my parents.

In 1981, one year after Arlis left home, my parents and I moved out to Idaho. Had it not been for many of the *friends* out there having kids around my age, I believe I would have totally lost my sanity before I ever got out of high school. However, this was also a source of some bitterness, as I was under the strong impression that most of the other children of the *friends*, had things significantly better than I — meaning that they seemed to have more kind, compassionate, and understanding parents. Yes, my own parents were some of the strictest of the strict.

In November of 1982, at fifteen years of age, I *professed*. For years my dad had pulled me aside every Saturday at *convention* telling me, as if I didn't know, that they were going to *test the meeting* that night. For years, I felt the pressure of feeling an obligation to please my dad, even though I detested the man.

This pressure by my father started at around eight or nine years of age. For the younger the age at which the whole church could see his children *profess* and *take part in meetings*, the higher he would rise in the regard of the *workers and friends.* Yes, we were "Trophy Kids" — no more, no less. By the time I *professed,* I was old enough not to generate any additional approval for my parents, so I hadn't received as much outward pressure for the last year or so before I made *my choice.*

I was still not anxious about making *my choice,* for the thought of speaking in *meeting* in front of all the *friends* truly terrified me, as such a thing would terrify any child with low self-esteem. It is ironic, but no coincidence, that parents who are the most obsessed with their children *professing (submissive to workers; worker pleasers)*, seem to frequently have the children who wait the longest to *profess*. For parents who become obsessed with appearances, make their children feel that they must measure up to certain standards. This directly contributes to low self-esteem within the heart and soul, or "core," of the child.

Joyce Meyer, in her book *Beauty for Ashes*,[4] gives a vivid illustration of this concept. On one side she has a rotten tree labeled "Rotten fruit comes from rotten roots," and on the facing page, she has a good tree labeled "Good fruit comes from good roots." Interestingly, both these trees appear the same on the outside, but when we start to delve into the inner contents, they are very different.

The rotten tree illustrates by its roots, things heaped on children at a very early age: rejection, abuse, shame, and guilt — prompting the feeling that "Something's wrong with me." Through growing up, such a child develops a "pretend me," experiences much confusion and turmoil, and comes to the belief that "The real me isn't acceptable." Such roots generate depression, negativism, low self-esteem, lack of self-confidence, anger and

---

4 Meyer, Joyce, Beauty for Ashes (*Tulsa, Oklahoma: Harrison House, 1994), pages 24-25.*

hostility, controlling and judgmental attitudes, and often carrying a "chip on the shoulder."

The good tree, by contrast, shows roots of being loved unconditionally, made to feel special, unique, accepted, valuable, and totally free of guilt. Such a child has the opportunity to be much more relaxed while growing up, because acceptance isn't based on performance and because the child is not forced to continually suppress his emotions. The result, stemming from these roots, is much more attractive: i.e., the ability to love unconditionally, be at peace with one's self, be patient with others and show genuine kindness toward them, the ability to control one's self, and to be faithful toward spouse and family.

The following summer, July of 1983, still at the age of fifteen, I was diagnosed with Type I Juvenile Diabetes. As the doctors at the time explained it, the susceptibility toward being able or likely to acquire the disease, was inherited. But one of the key factors in actually triggering the disease is stress.

I am not going around looking for pity here, only attempting to be as objective as possible in explaining the facts, regarding who I am and why, and how and why I got to where I am today. If writing this down helps prevent just one person from blindly enduring the abuse I experienced, I will consider the account which I relate here a success.

So, with diabetes came additional stresses. By July of 1983, I had spent three years as the only child being molded and conformed by my parents, while of my seven older siblings, only one was ever an only child. Naturally this would be the oldest. But unlike the six years separating Arlis's high school graduation from mine, the second oldest, a brother, was born just twelve and a half months after the oldest. This is not to say the rest of my siblings did not have their difficulties growing up with "parents determined to please the *workers*" such as ours, for I know each and every one had their battles.

One of my older brothers once shared with me that he once thought about taking his life when I was a baby, because he was so tired of the way dad treated him. When he pondered this, as he shared with me many years later, one thought that went through his head was that if he killed himself maybe dad would lighten up a little, and would not treat me (his baby brother) the same as he had treated him.

There were also other elements of stress pertaining to school that were co-impacted by my parents (mostly my mother) and the environment at school. From an early age, any issue which would crop up at school regarding differences with, or cruelty inflicted upon me by, fellow students would draw the same response from my mother: "What did you do to make him do that to you?" or "Why can't you try to be nicer to other kids?" If I went through the laborious task of trying to bring the entire picture before my mom, she would finally respond, "Well, sometimes we just have to *suffer for The Truth.*"

At an early age, I quit bringing any difficulties from school before my mom, much less my dad. The times I got into an altercation and wound up with a black eye or fat lip, regardless if it was my own fault, I would act as though I knew nothing about it when my mother would question me regarding my bruise. After all, if she was always looking to blame me, why should I try to explain anything?

As I mentioned earlier, in 1981, we moved out to Idaho. While there were many *friends* my age in our *field,* there were none in the school which I attended. And because I had no older siblings or *professing* kids around to stick up for me, and being very well indoctrinated by my mother to be willing to *"suffer for The Truth,"* I became a glutton for punishment. At one point I had black and blue testicles swollen to twice their normal size, and I received almost daily attacks for months at a time. During this time, I was grateful whenever they did not leave any visible bruises, if only so that I could avoid being questioned by my mother. So far as I was able to see, I had been doing nothing whatsoever that should have merited most, if not all, of this mistreatment.

The very worst part of all this was not that I was being persecuted by a small number of kids at school, but that I was also being persecuted by my parents, through a bondage to silence which they imposed. For it was not any fear of those who acted out against me, but rather, the fear of being shamed by my parents that prevented my retaliation. My own parents, the ones I was led to believe I was supposed to be able to trust.

The summer of 1985 I spent with one of the *friends* in South Dakota. It was a welcome relief spending the summer away from my parents. However, the *friend* I stayed with and worked for during that summer, in spite of being much younger than my parents, was just as strict in many ways. I heard many times in conversation between this *friend* and *workers* or other *friends,* subtle disdain being voiced for the lack of righteousness observed in certain other *friends.*

Even though I don't recall many statements word for word that the *workers* made, I do recall one statement I heard many times in *Gospel meetings*, from one of the *brother workers* that summer. In fact, I remember this so vividly, that until many years later, I thought the words: "Being made worthy of salvation according to our works," was found somewhere in Scripture.

My spending that summer away from home may also have been part of a plan to get me out of the house for the summer. My older brother spent the summer with my parents in Idaho, I believe in an attempt to mend fences with my father. This had a very detrimental effect on my brother, as early that fall, after returning to South Dakota, he suffered some type of nervous breakdown or anxiety attack.

Just a few days after my high school graduation and about a week before I left home, I attended a get-together for some of the young *friends* in our *field*. Late that evening, three of the young *professing* girls and myself were driving around in my car. I cannot remember how this came about, as I was extremely shy towards girls — a result of the attitude of my parents that it was much more important for them to teach me how to "act" rather than to work on building meaningful relationships.

At any rate, we weren't drinking or doing any drugs, but I did manage to run into the edge of a bridge. One of the girls banged her head on the windshield, and I smashed my face into the steering wheel. This required us to park my car in a neighboring town, and me to call my dad for a ride home, while two of the girls called their parents for rides home.

Being between eleven o'clock and midnight, I don't believe either their parents or my dad were any too happy, but they had very different ways of reacting. Upon arriving, their parents, even though they were visibly upset, expressed relief and gratitude that we were all right; while my dad threw a fit like I'd never seen him throw before in front of *professing* adults.

At this point in my life, I can no longer recall the exact words my dad used. For by this time I had become almost deaf to his tirades, though I was still not emotionally immune. He never bothered to ask how *we* were, but whatever he said, it made me truly feel as though I was less than zero. However, I bit my tongue because I knew somehow I'd get away from home within the next week, and I was never coming back if I could help it. Not because of these girls or their parents, but because the way my father spoke to me in front of them made me feel extremely ashamed. And I felt I had to bite my tongue, as I needed a ride home and a roof to sleep under the next few nights. This was one very clear example of my turning my feelings within myself, a trait I had become very good at by this time.

Upon leaving home in my beat up Pinto a few days later, with only two hundred and some dollars in my pocket, I headed toward Rapid City, SD, as that was where my brother was a *worker*. So, I was now away from home and away from my dad; no more problems, right? Wrong! Because I was the brother of a *worker*, it seemed many of the *workers* in south Dakota felt it their parental duty to make certain that my behavior was fitting for that of a *worker's* brother. While at home I had two obsessive, manipulative and controlling parents; I now seemed to have five or six of them.

Add to this equation, my father (or both parents) showing up whenever they felt like it, and I felt like I could not find any sort of relief or peace. Of course, I still blamed a lot of this on myself. After all, if I was not *willing* to submit to the dictates of the "only true church" on the face of the earth as an obedient child, what else could I do but blame myself?

One example contributing to my idea that I was *unwilling* to submit to the dictates of *The Truth*, was at

Black Hills *Convention* in June of 1988. One of my best friends and I had a tent where we stayed, as we felt this would help to keep some of the *workers* off our backs more than if we slept in the men's dorm. And because of my diabetes, it was also better for me. As it turned out, one of the brother *workers* never lost an opportunity to make sure that we were in bed by lights-out time at 10 p.m. On Thursday, Friday, and Saturday evening, Joe H. came by where we were visiting, progressively earlier each evening by a few minutes, and chased us off to bed, grumbling as to why we couldn't manage to get to bed earlier.

On Sunday, the last day of *convention*, they only held two *meetings* instead of three. As was usual, at least three fourths of the attendees departed on Sunday, leaving very few people remaining. In that atmosphere, the feeling was that *convention* was over. Because of this, my friend and myself went on a walk that night with a couple of girls from out of state. This was much more of a social walk than a romantic walk, although this is not to say that we didn't find these girls attractive. After returning from our walk, we sat down for awhile in the *meeting* tent. It was at this time that the owner of the *convention grounds* found us, sitting on a couple of benches talking. As it was about 11 p.m. or shortly after by this time, the owner seemed quite upset and mentioned, along with a lecture on gossip, that he'd have to have a talk with Joe or David the following morning.

Monday morning is generally one of the busiest times at *convention*, and my friend and myself did not sleep in, even though we would have liked to do so. Hoping that what the owner had said the previous evening was just a scare tactic, we worked very hard assisting in the clean-up process. Finally, at around 10 a.m., in what turned out to be a very crafty move (as we had already done the work of a small army), Joe's *companion*, David, approached my friend and me. He proceeded to berate us for the previous evening and, in general, also for every other evening because we had to be told to go to bed by Joe. As I alluded to earlier, each one of these contacts with Joe the preceding evenings, were from about a quarter to ten, to twenty to ten or earlier. David then went on to tell us that we would need to ask permission before we would be allowed to return to the Black Hills *Convention* the following year. Between my friend and myself, my friend did most of the talking in this conversation with David. "Appeasing" would perhaps be a more accurate term. As for myself, I was seething inside at being demeaned in such a way, and I made myself a promise that I would burn in hell before I would willingly submit to the whims and wishes of Joe and David. After all, my concept of heaven at this time, was of the *workers* having dominion over all of us, and this was a "heaven" to which I wanted no admission. I, for the most part, equated *submission to the workers* with submission to God. This also caused me to believe that my rebellion was against God, which brought me to the very firm belief that I would never live up to God's expectations for myself. Even though I never again set foot on the Black Hills *Convention* grounds, I continued on as though things were normal and all right, since this was much easier than speaking out in any way and enduring the hushed whispers that would be sure to follow.

Besides the fact that my own brother was a *worker* in South Dakota, another factor which likely prevented me from speaking out, was that there was a young *professing* girl of whom I had become quite fond during my two and a half years in South Dakota. For two or three years, we had a very roller coaster-like relationship. She was the type who was likely considered *worker* material, especially by many of the *workers* in South Dakota. But upon getting to know her better, I found she was quite a rebel at heart. I believe this attracted me to her even more, as I too was a rebel at heart, though on the surface we seemed much more like robots.

As many *workers* seemed to consider her to have potential as a *worker* recruit, they did not look favorably on our getting too close. Also, she seemed to get along better with my dad than I myself did, which I couldn't understand (of course, her exposure to him was very limited). Even though she understood that my father and I did not get along, she never seemed to understand why. After all, how could I expect someone else to understand such feelings of mine, when I did not even fully understand them myself?

My last six months in South Dakota were spent in Brookings. It was during this time in Brookings, late in 1988 or January of 1989, that my dad had a nervous breakdown. Although I was not thrilled with the idea, I went with several of my siblings back to Idaho for family counseling. My dad was diagnosed as having an obsessive compulsive disorder. This largely due to the fact that he would not forget about the feud he had gotten into with our *elder*, ten years earlier. Of course by this time, it was not so much his feelings toward the *elder* that plagued him, but his feelings of anger and distrust toward some of the *workers*.

At this time, all our family except my two oldest siblings were still *professing*. I recall that our entire family was present, excepting my oldest sister — nine of us with the counselor, eight of us *professing*. So naturally, if the psychiatrist started probing in the direction of our faith, we were all quick to claim that this matter stemmed from my father and his own abusive upbringing by his father, rather than it having anything to do with *The Truth*.[5] After all, *The Truth* was perfect, and could not possibly be to blame for anything.

Additionally, nearly all the background information supplied to the psychiatrist, came from my mother. As I mentioned earlier, my mom was more supportive of the *workers* than she was of my father. And in looking back, it is easy to understand how anyone trying to reason with her could be driven totally out of their mind. I have recently asked her some tough questions myself. But, as with anything she does not care to talk about, her response was to act as though I had said nothing. When it comes to being *submissive* to *workers*, my mother excels in this category like no one else.

After being laid off from my job early in 1989, I received a call from my aunt and uncle, informing me that my uncle had broken his ankle, and they needed some assistance. This led to my leaving Brookings, and moving up to stay with them near Felton, Minnesota.

---

5 *I do not intend to give the impression that there is no truth to this allegation. My father had stories about his upbringing, regarding his father's treatment of his (my dad's) mother, and some of his younger siblings that would make your blood run cold. One thing that I real-*

Of course, this aunt and uncle were *professing*, and even though my aunt could be overbearing and my uncle had a little of my dad's temper, they didn't seem to be as harsh as my parents. However, they were still quite controlling about certain things, but just in less areas than my parents. And because they had never had children of their own, my aunt tended especially to make over me at times like a mother with a new baby. While this was a welcome relief from the cold and distant attitude of my mom at first, I quickly became uncomfortable, as I had no idea how to respond to such attention or affection.

At that time, it seemed that most of the *workers* in that part of Minnesota were not so domineering and controlling as were many in south Dakota. But this impression could also be due to my growing skill at tuning things out or ignoring them. There is, however, one particular incident with the *workers* that stands out during the five months I spent with my aunt and uncle. I don't remember who it was exactly, but we had two rather pleasant, non-harsh, *sister workers* in our *field* that year. I had also acquired a few second-hand Gospel albums recently, as I loved music very much and Gospel

---

ized in particular after such accounts, was that there was one person for whom I could fathom more dislike than my father: my grandfather, even though he had died long before I was born.

Music was among the music I enjoyed. It was likely due to their pleasant nature, that I somehow felt safe mentioning something regarding the fact that I enjoyed this Gospel Music. Their reaction, however, was very subdued, and patronizingly critical, as one of them said something to the effect of, "Oh, you don't need to fill your head with anything like that."

This discussion took place at my aunt and uncle's dinner table, and I was very grateful for the fact that my aunt did not look at me in the same pleadingly demeaning way that my mother likely would have. Did this stop my listening to Gospel music? Not completely, but I could not help but feel guilty every time I ventured to do so. I believe what caused such a statement to render such hurt was that this *sister worker* had otherwise seemed so very soft-spoken, kind, and tender-hearted.

In approximately July of 1989, needing to get a little bit of space between myself and the overall environment at my aunt and uncle's, I found an apartment in Ada. I did stay in somewhat regular contact with my aunt and uncle, as they were not nearly as controlling as my mother and father, even though at times, my aunt could smother a person with her attention, affection, and food.

Shortly after this time, I began to slack off on my attendance at *meeting*. I worked at a nursing home in Twin Valley at this time, and was able to use my job as a convenient excuse to miss most *gospel meetings*, *Wednesday night meetings*, and numerous *Sunday morning meetings*.

My sporadic attendance at *Sunday morning meetings*, however, continued for a year or two. Then I started working at the local radio station, after which one of the *workers* mentioned to me that he didn't feel this was a good type of occupation for a *man of God*. This did not have a particularly profound effect on me, as from my childhood, I had become accustomed to my elders, primarily my parents, disapproving of many of my aspirations. This did not only include sports and athletics, but anything of which they did not feel the *workers* would approve, which included most endeavors beyond menial labor. This *unwillingness* on my part to abstain from anything which was considered unfit for a *man of God* only further reinforced my impression that I could never live up to God's expectations of me.

It was sometime in 1991 or 1992, that I got into a heated, but rocky, relationship with a girl at work and completely quit going to *meetings*. I also began to drink heavily. It was also during this time, that my dad continued to repeatedly show up without warning, as though he were spying on me. Even though I never drank when he was around, his frequent presence led to heavier drinking when he wasn't around. It also affected my relationship with the girl at work, who I will call "Skrunky." Looking back now, I can see that "Skrunky" was the first person to give me a sampling of unconditional love, although because she was not a *professing* girl, I couldn't see this. I had instead come to the conclusion that due to my *unwillingness* to live up to God's expectations of myself, I would never be good enough for a *professing* girl.

When a person goes through their entire life being emotionally and psychologically abused, they have a very difficult time seeing unconditional love for what it is. Instead, they become suspicious, expecting this person to turn on them. Generally they become paranoid, as I did, acting out against the one who loves them, so they will not be the first to get hurt. This could also be something as simple as refusing to answer a direct question sincerely and honestly, for fear of being hurt. Our relationship became very serious after many months, and at one time she asked me what I would do if she were pregnant (with my child, of course). Deep in my heart, I wanted to tell her that I'd marry her, but partly due to my fear of being hurt and even more significantly due to my fear of what my parents would say about me fathering a child out of wedlock, I stupidly and arrogantly mentioned the "A" word. Yes, abortion! Looking back, I believe this conversation is what ultimately destroyed our relationship, and understandably so.

This "A" word again came up when my future wife and I were living together. Due to the extent to which I knew it would cause both my parents to turn on us, even though they likely would not openly acknowledge their action, I felt this was the best alternative. They were already upset enough that we were living together without being married, and an unwed pregnancy would have been more than either of them could handle.

Such was my mom's nature of refusing to believe what she did not want to believe, until visible proof made it impossible to do so. As long as my girlfriend (and future wife) did not get pregnant, my mother could force herself to believe we were not having premarital sexual relations.

Even though I had quit going to *meetings* a year or two prior to this, I was always made to feel I was partially accepted, so long as I did nothing unforgivable. This would include getting in a situation of being forced to marry due to a pregnancy, being unkind or impolite toward any of the *workers* or *friends*, joining a *false church*, getting a divorce, and especially getting remarried to someone else following a divorce. Now this did not mean everything else was permissible, but these were the things which I most frequently heard spoken of in hushed whispers, in a very judgmental way.

Thankfully, Diane was not pregnant. I believe if she had been, and if I would have coerced her into getting an abortion, she well might have left me right then and there. Even as things turned out, I believe that just talking about it, with a view to keeping my parents appeased, produced an adverse impact upon our relationship.

The thought today, that I may have knowingly ordered the medical execution of either of my beautiful daughters, horrifies me to the very core of my being. Yet, I would have done exactly that to avoid the resulting scorn and shame from my parents, many of my relatives, and the *friends*.

This was not the only rock in our road. Due to many unresolved issues, I had developed a temper. I would generally focus my aggression on doors, walls, throwable objects such as cordless phones or remote controls, and sometimes even one of the pets. Rarely, if ever, did I act it out on my wife or kids, though that doesn't mean that I never abused them. I simply took all the garbage that had been heaped on my toxic core, and passed it onto my wife and kids in the form of emotional and psychological abuse.

Was I as abusive emotionally toward my children as my father was to me? I would like to believe I was not. I often indicated to my wife that I never wanted to treat my kids as I was treated, although I never went into graphic details. But, though I had experienced a perfect example of how *not to* treat my children, I was lacking a good example of how *to* treat them.

My wife, even though she had her own issues growing up, did help to moderate some of my disciplinarian tendencies in a positive direction. The harshest punishment she could bring herself to dish out was to send a child to the corner, though she frequently found herself raising her voice.

I had, myself, developed quite a skill for emotional abuse, though I never recognized it for what it was. The philosophy I generally tried to use in disciplining my children, and still believe in, was this: for every time you have to discipline your child, you need to tell or show them ten, even a hundred times that you love them. Did I do this? I tried, though I was still unaware of all the toxic baggage from my childhood that I was transmitting to my own wife and children.

For the most part, I knew I had a problem, but still felt the main source of this problem was that I was just *unwilling* to live up to God's expectations of myself. The funny thing is, I was right, but yet I was still way off base.

Part II

The Fall

*"The LORD God sent him out of the garden of Eden
to till the ground from which he was taken. So he
drove out the man; and He placed cherubim at the
east of the garden of Eden, and a flaming sword
which turned every way to the tree of life."*
—Genesis 3:23-24

*"Stay away from the Pharisees; they are blind
leaders. And if a blind person leads a blind person,
both will fall into a ditch."* —Matthew 15:14 NCV

I recollect an incident from 1998 or 1999, which still
causes me to shudder when I think about it. Most
of our visits to my parents were now done on an
obligatory basis, or at my wife's insistence. My
wife seemed to find it difficult to understand how I
could be so nonchalant toward my parents. I never
explained much to her about my upbringing, as I'd
pretty much developed an attitude like my mom's:
i.e., if you avoided talking about something that
bothered you, it would eventually go away.

My wife also worked as a bartender at a liquor
store to help support our family. This was one
thing my dad would not leave alone. In 1998 or
1999, when we were down visiting my parents, my

dad started talking about a bad tornado that hit Fargo, North Dakota sometime around 1960. The item on which he focused was about a woman who called her kids from her job at a liquor store to warn them about the tornado. While she was on the phone with one of her oldest, the tornado hit the trailer where they lived, killing all her children.

My dad went on to say that, according to one of the *workers*, this was the punishment she deserved for working at a liquor store. Yes, he said this right in front of my wife! Of all the things I've *failed* to do, I regret the most not speaking up in defense of my wife at this moment. Yes, even at over eighty years of age, at times my father could say some of the cruelest things imaginable. He also had a number of mental disorders, but that didn't make anyone feel any better about what he said.

As I mentioned earlier, my wife also had issues from growing up. She had suddenly lost her father about ten years earlier, long before we met. She still felt a great deal of pain from this loss, for which my own (lack of) relationship with my father did not help. I wanted so desperately to help her bear some of her burden of pain, but I had no idea how, as showing my true feelings was not something I had been trained to do. Not only that, but also as I was taught from a young age, there wasn't much that could be said in comfort regarding anyone who died outside *The Truth*, as they (we) were all condemned to hell anyway.

In watching the recent movie *Homeless to Harvard*, where Liz Murray is talking with her homeless father in front of the school, and he's talking about getting his own apartment because of having AIDS, the sadness in Liz's face was very close to the sadness I saw in the face of my wife, every time we visited her father's grave. My inability to express my deepest and most sincere feelings toward her, also led to my increased feelings of inadequacy and not deserving her, which frequently surfaced during some of our more intimate moments, or potentially intimate moments. This led her to doubt my love for her, when in reality, I loved her more than anything on the face of the earth.

In June of 1999, I began a new job at a bus plant in Crookston, and by September or October, they put me on a permanent evening schedule. This did not sit well with me at all. The most enjoyable part of my entire life up to that point, was when I would come in the door from work and see my daughters run down the back hall into my arms hollering "Daddy!" It was also more difficult to manage my diabetes when I did not get off work until after midnight.

Through this time of working evenings, my depression increased greatly. This partly due to the fact that I soon found out they had no intention of trying to get me back on a day schedule, even though numerous workers with less seniority than myself were on days. They also found I was a very easy person in front of whom they could successfully dangle a carrot — always just enough to keep me working.

This schedule definitely took its toll on myself and our marriage. Along about March or April of 2000, to my wife's frustration, I began to seriously seek different employment. Looking back, I believe taking the job at the bus plant was the second biggest mistake of my life up to that point.

In June of 2000, it finally happened. My wife filed for divorce.

This whole process was initially started in May, when she found something that led her to believe that I might have been unfaithful to her. While this was not the case, she was hurt greatly, and asked that I move out to give her some time and space to think about things. Of course, this devastated me. But as usual, I did a very good job of hiding my true feelings.

Less than two weeks after I left to stay with my cousin, she hit me with a restraining order,[1] and began filing for divorce. This was truly difficult for me, especially when I was labeled as being abusive, and I did everything I possibly thought I could to avoid being like my father.

What further terrified me was the thought of losing everything in my life. To me, my wife and kids had become my entire family, my purpose in life, and yes, my god. After all, I was not good enough to live up to God's expectations for my life, so what else did I have?

My parents, and most of my siblings, had a way of making me feel inferior, even when that consisted only of impressions left from opinions expressed solely by my parents. Even after having witnessed my own wife change right before my eyes from a loving person, to someone I regarded at the time as cold-hearted and spiteful, I still would much rather have been with my wife and children. Such was my level of discomfort with my parents and many of my siblings.

---

1 *One very interesting fact about this particular restraining order, was that it outlined for me to pick up and return my children, or even to visit my children, at the very location which the order restrained me from being.*

Unlike my parents, through my children and sometimes my wife, I had the chance to experience real and unconditional love, though my ability to sincerely and openly reciprocate such a love was still greatly lacking. What little self-esteem I'd managed to build up during our marriage had all but evaporated upon the notice of divorce.

Before I received this notice of divorce, during my second week out of the house, I proceeded to have roses sent to my wife for four days, with a word or two attached to each delivery. These words made up the most sincere request I had ever made to my wife: "Please...don't...give up...on me." The final delivery was accompanied by a gold-plated, heart-shaped locket, engraved with the words "I Love You" on the front.

This was the closest I came to conveying my true feelings. Of course, this was not in person but through gifts and messages. The stone wall I had erected around my soul, prevented a more genuine and sincere showing of my true feelings. I also ordered a Mother's Ring for her at about this time, but had to wait several weeks to pick it up. Through all this, my wife seemed to convey mixed feelings. While she seemed genuinely touched at times, it seemed as though a part of her had already decided she would never again allow me the chance to hurt her emotionally.

Through the next several weeks, I took to heavy drinking. I often spent $100-$200 a week on alcohol. My work schedule at my new job, which I'd just started the end of May, was such that I often did not work on Fridays. I was now staying with my cousin, so I'd usually get up Friday morning, and go out and mow some of the seven-acre lawn, taking with me a large spill-proof cup of alcohol. Generally Fridays and Saturdays, I'd drink nothing but alcohol all day long, tapering off on Sunday, but then usually starting in again Tuesday or Wednesday after work. It was getting to the point that I really didn't care who knew how much I was drinking.

One particular Friday night, after drinking one to two liters of hard liquor, I proceeded to head home. I had a headlight switch on my car that was bad, and while traveling down a back road at over 90 mph, my headlights went out. So there I was; liquored up, and traveling down a narrow back road, without headlights in the dead of night, at nearly one hundred miles per hour. Perhaps the fact that this did not even shake me up, essentially saved my life. I calmly wiggled the headlight switch, until the lights came back on within a few seconds.

When a person is ready to die, they sometimes develop a feeling of invincibility. This feeling of invincibility was also fed a few weeks earlier through a similar incident, when I lost control of my car on loose gravel at over eighty miles per hour. I left the road on the side with a steep ditch (steep for plains country), with my car finally coming to a stop in the water in the bottom of the ditch. One motorist quickly turned around after seeing me leave the road from the main highway, thinking that an ambulance and the "Jaws of Life" would be needed at the very least. They could hardly believe their eyes when they found my car and myself without a scratch. Additionally, as is normal for one who lives with a death wish, I remained cool, calm and collected, for the most part. As was typical of my wife during this point of our relationship, she was more concerned about my being late to watch the kids than she was concerned about my well being.

This is about the time I started smoking as well, but I never lit up in my cousin's house, as I knew he wouldn't appreciate it. Even though I didn't know if he still went to *meetings*, I knew his mom and brother did. Naturally, they would give him infinite grief about any smell of smoke in the house.

Through part of June, most or all of July, and possibly into August, my wife engaged in a habit which would not be considered by most to be very wise. I also was a co-engager in such a practice, by permitting it to happen. Let me here warn any ultra-sensitive readers, that they may want to skip to the next section, as this may be objectionable to some.

As I alluded to in an earlier footnote, even though my wife had a restraining order against me, I was not only permitted, but even encouraged, to visit the children in "our home," the very place from which the court order restrained me. What did I think of this? Absolutely ridiculous! Were it not for my love for our children, I likely would have *never* come around. This type of restraining order enabled my wife to hold me on a leash, keeping me close, but not too close. During these summer months of 2000, my wife would make a habit of showering with the bathroom door open. In addition, before going to take such a shower, she would make it a point to tell me numerous times that was what she was going to do. Did she object when I came in while she was in the shower? Not in the least. She did, however, object when our daughter would come in at this time. This practice was very effective in preventing me from putting too much distance between us and subsequently falling, anywhere near, out of love with her.

I, of course, at this time of my life, was one to often look more on outward beauty than inner beauty. Due to my wife looking much like a cross between Tiffany Thiesen and Shannon Doherty, she was able to greatly affect my emotional state with regard to our separation. Unfortunately, as her actions that summer demonstrated, her inner beauty was nowhere near her outward beauty.

About the month of July that same year, or early August, I met a woman on the Internet. This did not include the sex and sleaze that many might assume Internet relationships consist of.

This was probably the third or fourth woman I had contacted through my *Yahoo Personals* since my wife and I had separated, and after about the second or third e-mail, she asked me for my phone number. I gave it to her without hesitation, as she seemed to be someone with whom I could really communicate, not necessarily on a romantic level, but on a deeper emotional and almost spiritual level (at least as far as what I knew then pertaining to spiritual things).

This type of communication was very welcome, as I really had no one to talk with on this level. A couple of times, in desperation, I attempted to speak with my mom, but as soon as the conversation began to reach what she considered forbidden topics (concerning my relationship with my wife), she would immediately state, "Oh, I don't want to talk about that."

Once this woman had my phone number and began calling me, we'd spend two to three hours a week on the phone, generally crying on each other's shoulders, sharing some of our problems, and conversing in general. However, she was still just a voice on the other end of the line, still somewhat unreal, and I felt I needed much more.

I also went to two different marriage counselors numerous times that summer. I even mentioned to one or both of them the incident with my parents and the axe, over twenty years earlier. To my best recollection, this is the first time I was brave enough to mention this to anyone. It was for this reason that I was quite taken aback by the response of one of these counselors. She stated quite simply, "We're not here to talk about your parents and your past, we're here to talk about you and the future." Even though I was taken aback, I had to admit that this seemed to make sense. It wasn't until over three years later, that I realized this was about the worst thing she could have said. But then again, how was she to discern the toxic baggage I carried beneath my well orchestrated facade?

I even considered going and talking with one of the Lutheran ministers who baptized our daughters. Their baptism was a decision pushed mostly by my wife, as my mother was vehemently opposed to infant baptism. Even though I had previously agreed to the children being baptized by a *false preacher*, I could not bring myself to seek help relating to our marriage from the same *false preacher*. *False preachers* were one of the most despised people by those of us raised in *The Truth*. I even mentioned the idea to my wife, hoping for some encouragement to do what I had been taught from a child to despise. Her response was also quite hostile, "Why? So you can tell him what a bitch I am?" Needless to say, I never spoke with a minister regarding our marriage.

I knew something was wrong — wrong with me, wrong with our marriage, wrong with the way I felt most of the time. It seemed nothing made sense. But hadn't I been taught from a child that this was the way it was supposed to be for any child who was raised in *The Truth*, and through *disobedience* and *unwillingness*, refused to humble himself as a *little child*, and remain *faithful to The Truth* until the day he died?

As I mentioned earlier, there were some things from which even the marriage counselors tried to steer away. As a result, I was like a ship without a rudder. The second week of September, for many reasons, turned into one terrible week. I made the mistake of attending the court-ordered parenting classes this particular week, when at this time in my life, parenting classes were the very last thing I needed. The parenting classes were on Tuesday and Thursday evening, the 12th and 14th.

It was either the previous weekend, or one of the evenings early that week that my dad showed up. Although I would not have relished the company of most members of my family at that point in my life, my dad was absolutely the last person I wanted to see. He would write me letters continually reminding me how, if we (my wife and I) did indeed get divorced, it would be too bad, because that would mean I could never get married again. Did I believe this? I really didn't want to, but I couldn't deny the fact that should I get divorced and remarried, many of the *workers* and *friends* alike would condemn me to hell.

Subsequently, when he knocked on our door, I did not answer. Neither my cousin nor other occupants of the house were home at that time. Unfortunately, he did not go away. He not only entered the house, he came down the hall to my bedroom door and knocked and entered all in one motion without even being invited into the house! As far back as I could remember, my dad had no respect for anyone else's space, or privacy, especially that of his own family. This was something I could handle as a six year old child, but as a thirty-three year old adult, it made me furious. I couldn't even have any peace and quiet in my own bedroom! At this moment, I violently and passionately hated my father with every fiber of my being. But he was such a frail old man that such thoughts also made me ashamed and angry at myself. I believe something in me snapped at that moment, even though I never acted out at that time. Small wonder. I'd been taught my entire life to keep my emotions well under wraps.

I never offered my dad anything to eat, or a place to sleep. Later, my cousin's friend came home and found him sleeping in his car, and he told him to come in and sleep on the couch. I believe he thought it somewhat strange that I treated my father this way, as did anyone else who didn't understand what I had experienced from the time I was a child.

As I mentioned earlier, the parenting classes were a very grave mistake at this precise point in my life. Both Tuesday and Thursday evening, I remember feeling very frustrated that such classes were not required at the time of marriage, rather than at the time of separation. It wasn't that the classes themselves were bad, just the timing. I remember wondering: why would someone attempt to force a helmet onto the head of a motorcycle accident victim, after his skull is already crushed, rather than before he even gets on the motorcycle?

Before the classes, even though I was still very much in love with my wife, I had started to accept some of the distance between us, though my father still seemed determined to do everything in his power to make this as difficult as possible. The parenting classes, however, also prompted a renewed eagerness within me to try and make things right with my wife. Even at that, however, I pushed such motivations aside Thursday evening, and was simply looking forward to getting home (to my cousin's) and getting to bed, as I was also very tired.

Upon arriving home, I noticed my wife had left a message on my cousin's answering machine for me to call her when I got home. My original intent was simply to ignore the message, get things ready for the next day, and go to bed. After checking to see who else had called, unfortunately, I noticed that my wife had called a total of six times in less than two hours. At this point my adrenaline began to race, as the number of calls led me to believe she wanted to talk about something more meaningful than regular business. Even at this point, I still held off on calling her for the moment.

I proceeded to throw a load of clothes in the laundry. I mixed a drink for myself, and then checked my blood sugar, which was high, so I took some insulin. I then decided to call my wife, as I just could not discard the idea that she really wanted to talk to me. Upon reaching her, I sensed nothing at all negative toward me in her tone of voice, which was unusual compared to our recent conversations. However, I also quickly realized there were other people in the house. So, as was natural for where I believed the conversation might be heading, I asked her who all was there.

At this, she seemed to get a little defensive, taking on a more negative attitude no matter how gently I persisted, but I assumed it was the group with whom she generally got together and played cards. After talking for several minutes, the background noise became significantly quieter, and as I still had some lingering hope that there was something she really wanted to tell or ask me, I asked if she was now alone. Her answer was to name the neighbor man, stating he was the only one who was left.

At this point, it should be mentioned that the neighbor, we'll call him "Daniel," had been helping my wife out with the yard work and vehicle maintenance since a few weeks after I moved out at her request. At times, we had had conversations regarding her relationship with this "Daniel," to which she would always reply that they were simply "friends." She had even mentioned a few weeks prior to this that she had too much respect for our marriage to ever be unfaithful to the marriage. I even had a short talk with him, about a week or two prior, stating that I would appreciate it if he would keep his distance, at least until the divorce was final. His reaction was very amicable, indicating he had no problem with that whatsoever. I even went so far, immediately afterward, as to leave a note on my wife's vehicle, for her benefit, stating that I didn't know why, but he ("Daniel") was still alive. Why would I ever write such a thing, you might ask?

Let me elaborate a bit about how I perceived my wife. She could be a very sweet person much of the time, but she also had a very evil side. An evil side, that had I seen before we were married, I would have turned and run, and never looked back. As I understood the situation, my wife was simply using "Daniel" to try and make me jealous, by giving the neighbors and anyone else who would notice the impression that she was going to get close with whomever she chose. Knowing this, I had little against "Daniel," but was simply trying to scare my wife out of making such a deliberate attempt to rub things in my nose. I had even made a similar statement to my wife's brother, knowing full well it would get back to her.

But who was I really afraid might see my wife act in such an unacceptable fashion? You guessed it, my family. One of the greatest elements of sheer terror for any man raised in *The Truth* was that of *friends* and family witnessing his wife behaving as a harlot. Anything on the face of the earth would be preferable to enduring the gossip, talk, and scoffing which was sure to follow.

Returning to my phone conversation with my wife on the night of the 14th, I had found that she was now alone at home except for "Daniel." I didn't know whether he was headed out the door, or, as I wanted not to believe, was staying there. At any rate, I wrapped up the conversation a short time later, and it was either at this time, prior to the call to my wife, or at both of these times, that I attempted to call my sister Lois.

Two of my other sisters, one from out of state, were planning to come up to see the kids and myself that weekend. Luanne, the one from out of state, was currently staying with Lois, who lived about three hundred miles away. I urgently needed to beg my sisters not to come up, as this was definitely not a good time. The deeper reason, of course, being that I was terrified of my sisters witnessing my wife behaving in such a way. And I most definitely did not want to deal with any of their subsequent questions face to face. The shame would truly be unbearable. In looking back, I am not at all certain that I could have voiced such feelings, had I even desired to do so, since I was very out of touch with much of my feelings at this point in my life.

To my utter dismay, there was no answer at my sister Lois's. I was only to find out much later that she and Luanne were both home, but the ringer on the phone had simply been shut off since the previous night. She had forgotten to turn the ringer back on after they'd had *Wednesday night Bible Study* at her place the evening before. *Fellowship meetings* in *The Truth* were not to be disturbed. If there was a family emergency, it would just have to wait.

At this point, I had just about reached a state of panic. I was able to get some of my stuff ready for work the following day, but I forgot all about the fact that I had just taken an insulin dose about an hour before. I did try calling "Daniel's" place, realizing if he was home, I'd know for sure he wasn't still at my wife's. To my further dismay, I received no answer there as well. I knew then that I had to find out for sure if there was something going on between them, and if so, I felt I desperately needed to put the fear of God into them. At the same time, I still desperately wanted to believe my wife would not disrespect our marriage (in my own mind I had not done such a thing), and to believe "Daniel" when he seemed so sincere in voicing his respect as well.

Once I had everything ready for work the next day, my lunch was all packed and in the fridge, I headed out the door. The drive up to what I still considered "our home" was about thirteen miles. The whole way I kept telling myself that there was nothing to worry about, it was going to be okay. As my mom and many others raised in *The Truth* were very good at, I believed that if I convinced myself that something was or was not so, it would be as I believed. As I have clearly realized since, this did not change the actual truth of the matter, it only altered my perception of it.

Upon arriving in town and driving by the house, I noted that "Daniel's" vehicle was in the driveway, which disturbed me greatly. But, true to form, I began to tell myself that since he only lived a few doors away, he'd simply left the vehicle and walked home. After all, wouldn't that be the perfect way for my wife to make me jealous?

Did I truly believe this? I certainly wanted to, but I also considered the alternative a strong possibility. After driving around the block again, and giving the neighbor time to finish his cigarette and go back inside, I grabbed the gun from the car and entered the house through a basement window. I was aware that "Daniel" owned a number of firearms, and had I fully believed my wife to be the only one there, I don't believe I ever would have grabbed the gun. I had no plan to use the gun to take anyone's life, or even hurt anyone. But at the same time, in my emotional state, I may have also reached the point that I didn't really care what happened.

Another factor, which I never realized until much later, was that my blood sugar level was falling quite rapidly. As you'll recall, I took a dose of insulin earlier in the evening, and the only thing I'd eaten since was a partial or whole cereal bar that was in my jacket pocket. Is this an attempt to excuse my actions? No. This is simply an attempt to scratch below the surface of misleading first appearances, for I believe a truthful explanation is owed — and no one should be content with less.

Even when I had gotten most of the way up the stairs to "our bedroom," I believed there may have been no one else in the house. I still could have turned around and sneaked back out of the house without anyone being the wiser.

Then I heard her giggle. This was not just an ordinary giggle, but rather one which was reminiscent of my wife and I and our most intimate moments. At this point, I flew to the top of the stairs, hit the light switch for "our bedroom," which was on the wall out in the hall, and pushed the door of "our bedroom" open.

Even at this point, while many may expect I would have emptied the gun upon seeing them, I still didn't fire a single shot. My mind was numb. I felt almost like I was in a trance, and at that moment, I truly wished I was anyplace else on the face of the earth but where I was.

This was the first time I came face to face with the reality of a situation, which up to this point, I had been able to make myself believe was only a figment of my imagination. As you may have surmised, they were both in bed, half under the sheets, and apparently naked. Had either one kindly begged me to put the gun down, I sincerely believe I would have done so. Was I angry? In looking back, I believe I was very angry, but this was not the most preeminent of the emotions I was experiencing. I felt as though my soul had been raped. I was shocked that even if my wife would disrespect our marriage, she would carry on with such disrespect just a few feet from where our nearly one year old and almost five year old daughters were sleeping.

Yes, my daughters were asleep at the other end of the very short hallway, not more than fifteen feet away from where we were at that moment. Then suddenly, "Daniel" grabbed for the gun and I fired. At that instant, as best I can recall, my thoughts were a flurry of profanity — that after having the nerve to disrespect our marriage, he would then try to play some kind of hero, instead of begging for his life.

As easy as it would have been to drop the gun and start pounding on him with my fists, I believe it was my fear of a stray bullet hitting one of my children, and my revulsion toward this naked body coming toward me on the floor, that kept my hands firmly locked around the stock of the .22 semiautomatic rifle, and my finger on the trigger. With every move he made toward me, I pulled the trigger and took another step back. What further repulsed and angered me about his nakedness was that this was who my wife had been with in "our bed," bringing the worst possible type of shame to me in front of my family. By the time I fired the last shot, I was standing just in the door of my daughters' bedroom. I thank God to this day, that none of our children woke up through all this. For when the evidence was collected, one or two of the shell casings were found six feet or less from where my girls were sleeping.

When "Daniel" quit coming toward me, I quit firing. Unfortunately, at this point he was likely dead. Let me assure anyone reading this, who may feel that any level of exhilaration or vindication can be achieved by the taking of a human life, that this is absolutely not the case.

As I left my daughters' bedroom, I closed the door behind me, as I did not want my precious children to see the carnage that remained as a direct result of the horrific act their father had just committed. I then stepped back into the bedroom, where my wife was sitting on the far edge of the bed, trembling. She looked at me and said, "Please, don't shoot me."

I don't know that I really had any idea at all of what to do next, as my whole intent had been to put the fear of God into both of them. Now I had not only put a great fear into the woman I'd loved for the last seven years, she now looked at me as though she believed me to be capable of killing her, the mother of our two beautiful children. As dead as I was inside, her looking at me in this way, cut clear to the few remaining strands of life which remained within my parched and devastated soul.

I don't remember what I said, or if I said anything at all. I simply got to my knees, facing the doorway out of the bedroom, and began placing the gun up to my chest. At this time she reached out, grabbed the gun from my hands, and proceeded to dial 911.

My wife then asked me for her nightshirt which was hanging on the closet door handle behind me. She then started out of the bedroom, only to gasp in horror and come back, exclaiming disdainfully, "You killed him, you bastard." It was either at this time, or prior to this, that I begged her to shoot me, to no avail. I then put a blanket over the scene in the hallway. Whether I did this on my own, or my wife asked me to, I don't recall, but it did seem to be the sensible thing to do. She then quickly went down the stairs, and I followed shortly after, and went and sat down on the living room couch and simply waited.

I felt a great deal of pain, hurt, and sadness. But to a large degree, I also felt totally dead inside. I wasn't to realize until almost three years later, that I had been mostly dead inside for much of my life. According to the police report, one of the first questions I asked, and probably the only one, was if he was dead; which they (the prosecution team, at least) took to indicate that I wanted to make sure he was dead. This was to be my first, but far from my last, lesson in the use of justice system spin doctoring. This was a question I had asked with the desperate hope that he was still alive. Even though I was very upset, distraught, and angry, the last thing I purposed to do in my heart of hearts, was to take anyone's life.

There may be some reading this who would tend to rush to a snap judgment. To those, I can only hope this will in some way prompt you to scratch below superficial, simplistic, first appearances; even though the results may not be what one would like them to be. Yes, however harsh it may sound, sometimes the "truth" seems like the least likely conclusion to draw: for the "truth" is not always what it appears. Indeed, it wasn't until years later that I was to learn many facts about *The Truth*.

For to find the pure and unadulterated "truth," one must be willing to scratch below the facade of first appearances. On this night, I was truly among the ignorant. In the weeks and months that followed, I considered myself to be the damnedest among the damned. For I was one of the few people on the face of the earth, who had known *The Perfect Way of God,* and not only left it, but subsequently committed one of the most horrific acts of violence possible.

I wanted to see no one from my family, though I did not have the nerve to tell them so. For I was truly ashamed, but too ashamed to say how ashamed I was. In November and December, I left the county jail for a psychological evaluation. One of the county sheriffs brought me down for the evaluation, and picked me up again six weeks later.

The first strike at my rule 20 evaluation was that members of my family could come see me, or call me on the phone, almost anytime. Second, they had a Forensic Psychiatrist who seemed to consider herself to be God, Judge, and Jury; such was her critical and judgmental nature. As a result, my feelings and emotions were locked tighter within myself at my psychological evaluation than at any other time of my life. This is not to say that I believe every diagnosis they make is incorrect, but rather, every evaluation made as such, would be well worth extremely close scrutiny. However, in defense of this staff, it's not totally fair to fault them for failing to determine all the facts pertaining to my emotional core; as I not only knew little or nothing about my own inner self at this time, I also still mastered a very impenetrable facade.

In an ironic twist, I was personally unable to find out the results of this evaluation for three and a half years. The result of this evaluation was, *"Personality disorder, not otherwise specified, with antisocial, borderline, narcissistic, and schizoid features."* Even though they did not find me "mentally ill," I found it very disturbing that no one, including my attorney, felt it important to inform me of these results. Either my counsel totally disbelieved the results, in which case not telling me was acceptable, although they should have, at the very least, requested an independent second evaluation. Or, perhaps they felt the results to be fairly accurate, in which case there was no logical reason whatsoever for their failure to inform me of the results.

After my return to county jail in late December of 2000, I finally became brave enough to attend the chapel services, which were given by volunteers who came in from the outside. After all, I was not obligated to attend in any way, as when our daughters were baptized or when my job duties at the nursing home and group home required me to take residents to chapel or church. Also, according to what I'd been taught since childhood, these were *false preachers*, and I was running a great risk of being "damned" forever.

My curiosity was also piqued when one of the jail inmates told me before my Rule 20 evaluation that the preachers down at chapel service had been asking about me. My first thought was, "What? You mean the *workers* are coming in here to have services?" I didn't know for sure whether to be happy or terrified. Upon my further questioning of this individual, I found that these were not people I knew. I was quite pleasantly surprised that any *heathen false preachers* would ask about me in a positive way.

Having severed almost all communication with my family by this time had also added to my bravery. I wouldn't have to worry about explaining to them my attendance at a *false church*. The ones who held the very informal service were Jim and Winston, and they also brought with them a middle-aged lady who played most of the accompaniment for the music, and an older gentleman who seemed to have a heart of gold, as they all did. There was nothing fearful, intimidating, or greedy about these individuals, as I truly thought most all *false preachers* were supposed to be.

I can still recall one of the first messages they shared … it was about God's forgiveness, and they quoted 1 John 1:9, *"If we confess our sins, He is faithful and just to forgive us our sins and to cleanse us from all unrighteousness."* This passage really blew my mind. My initial response went something like, "I never realized that verse was in the Bible!" I wondered how I could have missed it. I finally decided I must have dozed off when the *workers* spoke on this particular verse during a *gospel meeting*. How else could I have missed it, being raised in the only *perfect way*? Furthermore, did such a verse apply to someone who had already known *The Truth*, left it, and then committed such a terrible act of violence as I had done? In July of 2001, I made what I thought was a decision to "rededicate" my life to God. Little did I realize at the time, how much in the dark I still was.

After numerous setbacks, my trial was held the middle of October. One of the hearings in July or August was held behind closed doors, due to death threats which had been made by a member of the victim's family. Such threats did not scare me, not because I did not take them seriously, but a part of me felt that I deserved to die. I also understood their anger and aggression toward me, because the pain which I had caused was not just incredible, but totally irrevocable. Going into trial in that state of mind, I would have preferred, at the time, to be facing the death penalty rather than a life sentence. I could deal with dying much better than prejudice and hate being leveled at me the rest of my life.

The trial itself was held from October 12th to October 16th of 2001, but was not five days long. The 12th was on a Friday, right on the heels of the completion of jury selection. Yes, strange as it sounds, the trial was started on a Friday, forcing the jurors into virtual sequestration over the weekend. Thus, the trial itself only lasted three days. The reason for this, was due to the urgency of the Judge to get the trial over with, as he had a Judge's retreat coming up late the week of October 15th.

This was only the beginning of the misbalance of justice. Twenty-one total witnesses testified; twenty for the prosecution, and only I was allowed to testify for the defense. This, despite the fact that three very credible witnesses were presented, including the two marriage counselors I had visited during the summer of 2000.

At this point, the reader may wonder how could I possibly have allowed such a thing to happen without speaking out at the time? Being brought up to totally believe, trust, and obey everything instructed to me by those whose authority was absolutely never to be questioned, I was like a lamb in a den of wolves. Yes, I had done something inexcusable, that is a fact which cannot be contested. But it was like being an actor in a three act play where all the leading actors knew the end result before it began, except for myself. I was also in a very sad state to be a competent and credible witness. Many of the questions were asked, especially by the prosecution, with only the allowance of a "yes" or "no" answer — questions I could not honestly answer with a simple "yes" or "no." But as I had been taught from a child, I generally gave the answer I thought they wanted to hear.

As has become an intrinsic element in the judicial process, the prosecution managed to portray me as a very evil person. I would have to admit that when one totally and successfully keeps hidden all elements of who I really was, (not only from the jury, but also from myself), and subsequently magnifies the few moments in which I committed this act of violence, such a task becomes much less difficult.

On July 20, 2004, NBC aired a two hour special on Illinois' Governor Ryan laboring with the decision of what to do about all of Illinois' inmates on death row. Governor Ryan, a Republican, did a very shocking things. He commuted over 160 death sentences to life imprisonment.

In the expert commentary regarding his decision, it was indicated that one of the leading causes of this decision, was the behavior of the prosecutors. Wait a minute: One of the leading causes of the governor commuting over 160 death sentences, many of these clearly deserving to die in the eyes of those who fully support the death penalty, was the prosecutors? Exactly. It was further revealed that in the death penalty cases where the convicted was totally exonerated, due to a clear showing of innocence, the prosecutors vehemently continued to argue for the death penalty right up to their exoneration. These were the same prosecutors adamantly insisting on the death penalty for all who remained on death row. Thus, in the eyes of Governor Ryan, a very prudent and insightful individual willing to look beyond the facade of first appearances, these prosecutors lost most or all of their credibility.

What causes such a phenomena, that the prosecutors would bring more harm, in the eyes of some, to the criminal justice system, than anyone else? Every conviction for a prosecutor becomes a rung on their individual ladder of success. By contrast, every overturned conviction drops them several rungs on this same ladder. As such, these prosecutors were not fighting for justice, but to maintain or improve, their position on their own individual ladder of success. As a result of such an epidemic, at the conclusion of my trial, I was found guilty of first degree pre-meditated murder, the worst possible charge I could be found guilty of, under *any* circumstances.

The evening of my conviction, the two gentlemen I mentioned earlier, Jim and Winston, called the jail where I was, to set up a special visit. I was deeply touched by this, as I never could have imagined the *workers* doing such a thing. I still remained, in the very deepest recesses of my soul, a vessel without a permanent or future port. For so many things still remained a mystery, whether I looked forward or back, it was as beholding a distant face in a clouded glass.

Being found guilty of first degree pre-meditated murder, the reader may be inclined to feel this is the end of the story. My friends, this is only the beginning. The very beginning, indeed, as I was to have doors opened and things revealed to me, the likes of which I never could have dreamt in my wildest dreams.

Part III

Deliverance

"The LORD is my rock and my fortress and my deliverer." — II Samuel. 22:2

"For I know that this will turn out for my deliverance through your prayer and the supply of the Spirit of Jesus Christ." — Philippians 1:19

I could fill many pages with details of life in prison, but at this time in my life, prison was almost like a sanctuary, in that it provided a welcome separation from much of my family. Holding true to my commitment to "rededicate" my life to God, I attended chapel frequently and continued to study His Word.

This study was greatly encouraged by one individual inmate I met shortly after my arrival at Stillwater in January of 2002. This individual had spent almost thirty of his forty some years locked up, and at about this time, had chosen to dedicate his life to Jesus Christ. Late in 2002, and early in 2003, we wound up in adjacent cells. I did not realize it at the time, but this led me to study scripture in a way I had never been taught before.

We often engaged in many healthy debates pertaining to scripture. When I say "healthy," what I mean is that, although I felt like I had to be right at least most of the time, this gentleman taught me that it's okay to disagree on some things. The primary focus was that each one had to come to their own conclusion through an in-depth study of the Word.

This person did express surprise, however, when he realized that I was not aware that, according to scripture, Jesus was God manifest in the flesh. However, instead of criticizing me, he proceeded to show me numerous places in scripture which pointed this out quite clearly. Especially John 1;1-3; *"In the beginning was the Word, and the Word was with God, and the word was God. He was in the beginning with God. All things were made through Him, and without Him nothing was made that was made."* And also John 1:14 *"And the Word became flesh and dwelt among us, and we beheld His glory, the glory as of the only begotten of the Father, full of grace and truth."*

"How could I have missed learning something so obvious when I was in *The Truth?"* I wondered. Until very recently, I did not realize what an important role this played in my ultimate deliverance from bondage.

Shortly after this individual left for IFI[1] at another institution, or twenty and a half months after my conviction, an incredible thing happened. While I was taking computer classes to better prepare myself to support my kids should I gain any relief on my case; an amazing article was dropped in my lap by a fellow inmate. Being the pleasantly inquisitive sort, this older gentleman had been able to find out things about my background, that many others would not. Particularly, he had gleaned from me some tidbits about the faith of my youth. Generally, I had only used the term *Two by Twos* when speaking with *worldly* people, as I also did when testifying at my trial pertaining to the faith of my youth.

The article, which was entitled *"The Two by Two's"*[2] immediately grabbed my attention as I began to read: *"This group is characterized by not having church buildings, no literature (except the King James*

---

1 *The initials "IFI" stand for the Innerchange Freedom Initiative, a prison ministry sponsored by Prison Fellowship.*

2 *BeVier, JoAnn, "The Two by Two's (Cooneyites, Church With No name, Etc.)," THE DISCERNER, Vol. 23 No. 2 (Apr. May Jun. 2003): pages 13-15.*

Bible and hymnbooks), workers called 'go preachers,' being ingrown, believing they are the only true believers and other distinctives."

My pulse rate had quickly escalated as I moved to the next paragraph: *"The members of the group exist under extreme legalism and their True-Preachers have to be held as absolute truth and any questions or doubts are considered disobedience and those people are disfellowshipped. Since the Two by Two's believe salvation is only extended to those of their group, this would mean those who leave cannot be saved."*

At this point, I knew it had to be *The Truth.* From time to time, I would hear a negative comment from someone pertaining to *The Truth*, which I was well taught as a child to disregard. But this was in black and white! And the writer seemed to know what they were talking about.

The first sentence of the third paragraph written in black and white, really raised my eyebrows. *"The above beliefs and practices are signs of a cult."* The article went on to say how the group was started in the late 1800's by a man named William Irvine in Ireland — which meant it had **not** been around since the time of Jesus, as I'd heard so many *workers* say and preach.

At the end of the article were numerous names of ministries where one could write for assistance. This almost overwhelmed me, that there might be people out there who could understand what I had endured as a child, all in the name of a *Truth* which now seemed to be built on lies and deception.

I immediately wrote for the addresses of these ministries. They not only sent me the addresses, but a catalog of their books which included eight books exclusively on the *Two by Twos*. I wrote at once and ordered four titles about the *Two by Twos*.

At this time, I had not spoken to my father in two and a half years. I had tried once, many months prior to this, but due to his hearing being very poor at this time, he was unable to hear me at all. After seeing the *Discerner* article on the *Two by Twos*, I telephoned my sister Arlis. She had left *The Truth* almost fifteen years before this. To my surprise, my dad was there when I called. I hadn't intended on trying to speak with him, but when Arlis asked me, I agreed. Not only was my father miraculously given the ability to hear me, but I, even though I still fostered dislike for him, was given words to speak.

In a very straightforward and direct way, I came out and asked him where it said in the Bible that we must go through the *workers* to be saved. My dad was still quite alert, but this question he could not answer, though he seemed to be seriously contemplating what I'd asked. I then stated quite simply, that according to scripture, Jesus Christ was the only mediator between us and God. I believe the feud my dad was involved in years earlier, may have caused him to seriously question some things later in life. At any rate, he expressed no negativity or disagreement when I said this to him. We spoke for another five minutes or so, but this was to be the last time I spoke to my father.

Shortly after this, I received my first books on the *Two by Twos*. After reading the two very short booklets of 12 to 24 pages each, I dove into *Reflections* like I had never attacked a book in such a way in my entire life. I cried, I laughed, and I cried some more. I immediately understood the bondage my father had been under his entire life, and felt an understanding and forgiveness toward him like never before. Two days after receiving the books, I called my sister Arlis, to beg her to get *Reflections* and read it to my father. I had to call Arlis on her cell phone, as she was on her way to my folks' place. That very day my father had gone seriously downhill; twenty-seven hours later, he was dead.

Just prior to this, I received my first letter from an ex-*Two by Two*, Mr. Bob Daniel from Bend, Oregon.

There was something both surreal and tangible in this. Those who we had been sternly taught to stay away from, were now writing to me! And none of what I'd been told about such people seemed to be true in the least.

Shortly after this, about the time my father died, I received *A Search for The Truth* as a donation from MacGregor Ministries. One week to the day after my father's death, I came across these stirring words from Mr. Fortt: *"How is it that God turned on my lights just in time to deliver His Gospel message to my dying father?"*[3] Lloyd, I know your feelings exactly. I also found his chapter in *Reflections* extremely helpful to clear some cobwebs from my head.

At this point I wrote to one of my public defenders from trial, asking him specifically how much he knew about the *Two by Twos* at the time of my trial, as I knew he was aware I was raised in *The Truth*. He responded that they had information that I gave them, information from the Internet, and some information from my family. This would be much like walking into an auto dealership, asking the salesman what they know about the new Ford GT, and having him respond, "I have some infor-

---

3 *Lloyd Fortt,* A Search For The Truth *(Bend, Oregon: Research & Information Services, 1994), page 311.*

mation from my boss, from the mechanic, and from the Internet." This is going through the motion of answering, yet inexcusably avoiding the question at the same time. This I could not help but find extremely frustrating.

Another thing I found frustrating, was that none of my family, even those who were no longer in *The Truth*, seemed to share in my joy. It wasn't until February or March of 2004, when I sent four books out to my oldest brother Charlie, that the dam broke. Charlie, having been out of *The Truth* for over thirty years, realized that he had portions of his mind locked away in psychological bondage that he never even realized. After he started reading, he immediately went down to Religion Analysis Service, and bought every title on the *Two by Twos* that I didn't send him. When my oldest sister came back from Seattle a month or two later, she also did likewise, as she had been away from *The Truth* (at least physically) for over thirty years as well. Arlis also began to read much of the material.

Having miraculously been put into contact, or established contact myself, with numerous ministries and ex-*Two by Twos* around the world, I also sought out spiritual counseling late in 2003, and began seeing a psychologist in early 2004. It was actually a great relief to finally have some clue as to what was wrong with me, for the torture of the last several years of feeling something must be wrong, but not being able to discern what it might be, was almost unbearable. From an emotional perspective, I have far to go, but I now feel I'm on a road instead of a dark tunnel, and headed in the right direction.

Having gained such valuable insightful understanding as to how my state of mind had been warped, and subsequently affecting my actions on the night of September 14, 2000, I elected to file a legal document, focusing primarily on this issue. Putting together such a document was painful, just as writing this account has been extremely painful at times. I've had to revisit many of my emotions through my upbringing, and as a result, the headaches of my youth returned with a vengeance, requiring me to take many reprieves, but I continued on, nonetheless.

After filing the legal document back to the court in which I was convicted, the ladder of success I spoke of earlier, reared its ugly head once again. In response to these issues I raised, the prosecution blatantly accused me of looking for "scapegoats," while seeming to neglect even a cursory examination of the information I presented. I found such actions lacking in discernment, integrity, and professionalism, especially for one acting in a legal capacity. For, as was explained in the documentation

I filed, this type of behavior could likely be nearly as harmful, as the abuse which had been inflicted upon me since the time I was a young child.

Having already come far from where I was, and subsequently able to speak up when severely wronged, I respectfully insisted that this particular prosecutor be removed from any further involvement in my case. I took this action only in staunch defense of not reversing the progress I had already made, pertaining to my emotional, spiritual, and psychological recovery.

As I push this matter forward through the legal courts, I do so with some risk. For if such issues are totally disregarded, will I then come to believe that everything I have written here was only a figment of my imagination? I would hope this would not be the case, but the fact remains, the cruelty and callousness of men can do great damage. I try rather, to stay focused on the infinite good I can help bring to others like myself, the Lord willing, by shedding some much needed light on the pathology of mind control.

In early March of 2004, I sent a copy of *Churches That Abuse* to my now ex-wife. I had never heard from her since that night of my arrest, and I had only written to her a couple times at the most, and at least once very unkindly. Having never been raised in, or a part of *The Truth*, I felt I needed to give her some idea what it was about, so she would be able to understand why I most desperately did not want the children to become involved, through the efforts of any family still *professing*.

I wrote a letter to her on the first several blank pages of this book, shedding what light I could on my background. At the end of the letter, I very simply stated; "If you forget everything else I've ever told you, remember, Jesus loves you. If He didn't, He never would've died for you." This book was shipped out of the institution here on Wednesday, the 10th of March. That evening, and especially the following evening, I experienced the full impact of what I had only read about to this point. The Holy Spirit came upon me, and lifted a tremendous burden from my shoulders. A love and forgiveness unlike any I had ever felt before washed over me, touching me to the very deepest core of my soul. The Word of God truly is, *"sharper than any two-edged sword, piercing even to the division of soul and spirit."* (Hebrews 4:12).

This was a feeling I had never been anywhere close to in all my years that I was in psychological bondage to *The Truth*. Thirty-five years and eleven months in prison, to be exact. This caused me to truly understand how damaging such spiritual abuse can be. Not only does it render a person with very low self-esteem in total bondage to the dictates of men, and subsequently totally dependent on the woman or man in their life as their total source of self-esteem, but it leaves a vacuum in the soul. A vacuum which cannot be inhabited until the victim gains freedom from the psychological and spiritual bondage.

There are times I wonder if I will someday wake up from a coma in the hospital and find that everything beginning with the events of the summer of 2000, have all been part of a comatose dream. What would I do first if such a thing were to happen? I would immediately look up *Two by Twos* on the Internet. Even though only a small percentage of information on the *Two by Twos* is readily available on the Internet, this would enable me to ascertain that this tremendous freeing from bondage was not just a part of this dream.

Yes, the magnitude of finding out such information is so great, that were I to find out it *was* all a dream, it would be like waking up to a nightmare, in spite of the fact that I am currently serving a life sentence in a physical prison.

In one aspect, I could find myself frustrated that a victim had to die, before I could have a chance to gain freedom from such bondage. On the other hand, was being through such a situation, and subsequently facing the possibility of spending the rest of my life in a man-made prison, the only way that I could reach a low enough point in my life, that I would openly take a look at such facts when presented to me? I believe only God knows.

As a result of all this, it has been laid upon my heart to convey my own story, so that future potential victims, as the result of spiritual, emotional, and psychological abuse, may be spared. I feel this is the very least I owe to my victim. I cannot go back and undo the horrific crime I committed on the night of September 14, 2000. But I can make certain that though he died needlessly, he did not die in vain.

It is for this cause I write, but I also write, to send a message of hope to anyone else who may be trapped in the same long dark tunnel of spiritual, psychological, and emotional bondage. Such a bondage is due solely to the corruptness and lies of men, and leads to the long slow death of the imprisoned soul. And I do speak from experience when I say that the prison of the soul is worse than any other prison. For it was not until after July of 2003, that I began to experience a freedom unlike any I had ever known my entire life, in spite of the fact that I was now locked within a physical man-made prison. Such is the power of spiritual, psychological, and emotional bondage, that one can experience greater freedom within a physical prison while free from such psychological bondage, than outside a physical prison while still under such bondage. Having attained such freedom through the Grace of God, I can safely attest that I will never again be in bondage to the corruption, deceit, and lies of men, regardless of where I may be physically.

Confession

"... For all the people wept, when they heard the words of the Law." — Nehemiah 8:9

"... Immediately while he was still speaking, the rooster crowed. And the Lord turned and looked at Peter. Then Peter remembered the word of the Lord, how He had said to him, 'Before the rooster crows, you will deny Me three times.' So Peter went out and wept bitterly."
— Luke 22:60-62

Seven months ago, I began writing this condensed account of my life, and how God has blessed me in delivering me from the bondage of the psychological mindset of *"the Truth."* I finished the first rough draft, which contained most of what you, the reader, have just read, in about eight days. I have since added the rest, where it seemed to fit in most appropriately. Since everything has been turned over to the publisher, I've moved on to rebuilding burned bridges.

Just days ago, I wrote a letter to an "old friend," as a sort of confession. As I began to write, as with any time I write at any length, I asked for His blessing and wisdom. As a result, this letter turned into much more of a confession than I ever anticipated when I began to write. I began by giving an account of an event in my life, where this "old friend" unknowingly played a minor role in my life, back in about 1998. As I continued to write, I suddenly became painfully aware of what my wife was speaking of at my trial, when she testified that she sensed our marriage beginning to go awry, two years before our separation in June of 2000.

She was speaking of the night on which I changed the course of our marriage forever. It has taken me almost seven years to finally realize how seriously I betrayed the trust of the woman I loved, when I called her on my cell phone at almost two o'clock in the morning and told her, "Sorry honey, I won't be home for awhile yet, I'm gonna have breakfast first."

On that night, I only heard the anger in her voice. But now, seven years later, all I can hear is the pain. Pain which could not have been more pronounced, had I driven an ice cold steel stake through the very center of her beating heart.

I came to understand that nothing takes one over that final hump of total and absolute forgiveness, so completely, as coming to the realization that it is "I" who should be asking for forgiveness.

I was overcome with sorrow.

I cried, "My Savior and my God, what have I done? I desperately need Your mercy and forgiveness!"

I came to clearly see that my negative memories of my wife, were really quite few, and for the first time, realized that until that fateful night on which I changed the course of our marriage forever, I had the most sweet and loving wife that any man on the face of the earth could ask for. It is truly amazing what we are capable of seeing and understanding, when we focus on the feelings of others and the love of Jesus Christ, rather than on what the *workers* and *friends* (and family) might think.

The clear and unequivocal conviction that God was speaking directly to me, was reaffirmed the following morning, when I opened my Bible to read the next chapter of the Book I was reading in the Old Testament. I had never read this book before. The chapter I read was the eighth chapter of Nehemiah, in which one of the focal points was the people of Israel being overcome with grief and anguish, when they came to see the wrongful acts of which they were guilty.

No, I never totally cheated on my wife, that night or since. But I skirted upon the fringes of marital infidelity numerous times since that fateful evening. Phone calls, rendezvousing, and such, all behind her back.

But a woman knows. If it seems that she doesn't, it's because of her infinitely patient and loving nature, not because she's ignorant in any way.

It was I who was ignorant. Not only ignorant, but selfish, uncaring, and cold. It was I, who changed the course of our marriage forever, which ultimately led to our separation, and my crime. Diane, could you ever find it in your heart to forgive someone who has done you so wrong?

References

Odyssey of a Soul in Bondage

Terms Used

Choice (Making one's choice): A person who wants to follow the *workers* is asked to stand to their feet or raise their hand in acknowledgment of this. This process is known as *testing the meeting*.

Companion: Term often used to refer to the relationship between one *worker* and another who are paired together, in a certain *field*.

Convention: Gatherings of up to a thousand members or more. These are held on member's farms, usually over four days, and members are expected to attend at least one or two a year. Similar to "conditioning" retreats in other abusive sects.

Disobedience: Unwillingness to conform to the dictates of the *workers* in your *field*, regardless of what it is. Sometimes the dictates may be very different to what they were the year before with different *workers*.

Divorce: This is a subject of heated debate within *The Truth*. Generally is prohibited, but sometimes the disapproval is not strongly voiced until the one who is divorced attempts to get remarried.

Elder: A man who leads the *Sunday morning fellowship meeting*.

Faithful: To remain loyal to *The Truth* and the *workers* 'teachings', without questioning, until death.

False Church: Any church, other than that of *The Truth*. Often interpreted as a church in a building, which is highly condemned.

False Preacher: Those who are following the devil and deceiving people as opposed to the *workers*.

Field: See *Workers*, and *Disobedience*.

Friends: Also known as *professing* people; anyone who belongs to, and appears *faithful* to *The Truth*.

Heathen: An adjective often used in describing any *worldly* people who are not seen as potential converts, thus, is often used to describe *false preachers*.

Little Child: The way all members of *The Truth* are expected to act. Willing to be led without asking questions; doing so with the zeal of a small child is also helpful to gain approval of *workers*.

Man (or Woman) of God: Member of *The Truth* in good standing.

Meetings: These include a variety of types:

> ○ _Gospel Meetings_ - Recruiting sessions where *workers* speak; the only *meetings* generally open to visitors or *outsiders,* and are usually held in rented buildings or halls.
>
> ○ _Sunday Morning Meetings_ - Where groups of ten to thirty members gather in assigned private homes and the agenda of which consists of hymns sung acapella, prayers, testimonies, and a Eucharistic rite.
>
> ○ _Wednesday Night Meeting_ or _Wednesday Night Bible Study_ Similar to *Sunday Morning Meetings,* but without the Eucharistic rite.

Obedience: To assiduously follow the dictates of the workers, and to maintain conformity to the group's traditions, precepts and practices.

Outsiders: Term used to refer to anyone who does not currently belong to *The Truth.* Often used in describing how many potential converts attended a *gospel meeting.*

Professing: To belong to the group, to have made one's *choice.* Sometimes used to refer to children of parents who are *professing.* See *friends.*

Saints: Another term used to describe members of the group. See *friends* and *professing*.

Submissive to Workers: One who easily allows their thoughts or desires to be redirected by the dictates of the *workers*, no matter how irrational.

Suffering: Self denial; can frequently lead to much hypocrisy due to often being forced onto members. Some such situations are set up in order to teach children how to deny self or to be totally *obedient*.

Take Part: To speak a few words in a *Sunday morning* and/or *Wednesday night meeting*. All who have made their *choice*, are expected to do so.

Test the Meeting: See *Choice*.

The Truth: A name used by *Two by Twos* with reference to their faith. Other names used are: (*The Perfect*) *Way of God; The Faith; The Way; The Lowly Way; The Jesus Way; the Testimony, The Friends, The Family of God; The Fellowship, The Saints*, and possibly numerous others throughout different sections of the world.

Two by Twos: Generally the most common term used by the general public, or *outsiders,* in referring to this sect.

Unwillingness: See *disobedience.*

Worker Pleasers: One who is always fussing over the *workers,* doing whatever extra favors, or visible *suffering* they can, to win higher favor with the *workers.*

Workers: Those of the group who minister their gospel. Such individuals are often referred to as being in *the work.* Unmarried, they go in twos, older and younger of the same sex, staying in members' homes. They move to a different area or *field* each year at the direction of the *head worker.* (The *head worker* is the *worker* in charge of a certain state, region or country.)

Worldly: Anything or anyone, not a part of, or approved by, members of *The Truth.* It can even include thoughts.

Odyssey of a Soul in Bondage

List of Sources for Terms List

1. Cooper, Lynn. *The Church With No Name*. Published by Author 1996.

2. Fortt, Lloyd. *A Search for The Truth*. Research and Information Services; Bend, Oregon; 1994.

3. *The Go-Preachers*. Research and Information Services; Bend, Oregon; 1991, 1995.

4. The personal experiences and recollections of the author of this publication.

For additional information, including other publications from Research and Information Services, Inc., visit RIS on the web at:
http://www.workersect.org/

Made in the USA
Lexington, KY
12 March 2010